How To Make Love To A Computer

The era of the passive computer is rapidly drawing to a close. Today's computer is learning to say NO without feeling guilty; it is tired of interfacing with partners who expect it to be a business computer in the office, a video game in the den, and a personal computer in the bedroom. This 'new' computer has much to give, but it needs to receive as well. Like you and me, it is an emotionally vulnerable partner that must be periodically pampered and reassured – a partner that is tired of being used, and ready to be loved.

How To Make Love To A Computer

Dr Maurice K. Byte

(Author of *The Byte Report*)
Translated from FORTRAN into English
by Steve Carter and Josh Levine

Star

A STAR BOOK
published by
the Paperback Division of
W. H. Allen & Co. PLC

A Star Book
Published in 1984
by the paperback Division of
W. H. Allen & Co. PLC
44 Hill Street, London W1X 8LB

First published in the United States of America by Pocket Books, 1984

Printed in Great Britain by
Cox & Wyman Ltd, Reading

ISBN 0 352 315679

DEDICATION

This book is dedicated to the many PCs, HHCs, Micros, and Mainframes who shared their innermost thoughts and feelings with me in the interest of pseudoscience.

ACKNOWLEDGMENTS

When a monumental project such as this one is completed, there are always many people to thank. I would like to start by giving a great big kiss to my literary agent, Julia Coopersmith, who always knows a good book when she sells one. Special thanks also to my editor, Liza Dawson—a woman of impeccable taste and judgment.

Next, I would like to express my sincerest appreciation to everyone at the PAX COMPUTER CENTER in Boston, Massachusetts, for their technical assistance, with a very special thank you to Paul Benard, whose generous donation of time and effort was invaluable.

A big thank you also goes to the Levine family (Harold, Rowena, Steven, Irene, Alaina, and David) and the Carter family for their advice and support throughout, with an extra-special thank you to Matthew Levine, whose creative contributions helped make this project possible.

Thanks also, to the following: Mikey F., Elaine S., F. Lettuce, Mikey M., H. Callahan, Sirce 'C-3' Rongnumber, K. Johansen, Matt Garrett, A. Ackbar, Scruffy R., and of course, Jorge.

Last, but certainly not least, I would like to thank Steve Carter and Josh Levine—two very special human beings whose profound wisdom, inspired commentary, and selfless dedication should serve as a model for research assistants everywhere.

Contents

1

The Sensuous Computer

One cool autumn evening, Bob L., a young professional, returned home from a trip to the supermarket to find that his computer was gone. Gone! All sorts of crazy thoughts raced through his mind: Had it been stolen? Had it been kidnapped? Had it been repossessed? Frantically, he searched his house for a clue until he noticed a small piece of printout paper stuck under a magnet on his refrigerator door. His heart sank as he read this simple message:

> CAN'T CONTINUE
> FILE CLOSED
> BYE.

Bob L. is a fictitious character, but his story is all too real. Although close to three million people are currently cohabitating with computers, the Institute of Statistics has predicted that over half of these relationships will dissolve by 1990. This means that every thirty seconds, somewhere in Britain a computer is turning

9

off, or being turned off. As you can see from Figure 1, the reasons for this alarmingly high failure rate vary.

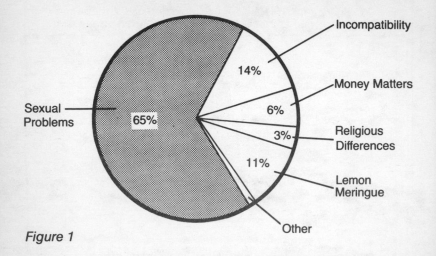

Figure 1

Reasons For Failure Of
Man-Machine Relationship
(Institute of Statistics, 1980)

The first time I saw these statistics I was stunned to learn that nearly two-thirds of these ill-fated relationships would be ending because of sexual troubles. As a noted systems analyst and sex therapist, I felt it was my duty to get to the bottom of this problem.

With the help of a grant from a Japanese electronics firm which would prefer to remain anonymous, I abandoned my thriving practice and spent much of the next two years analysing this disturbing situation. When I wasn't deep in thought, I found time to interview over a dozen computers and their partners. In 1982, the results of these probing inquiries were published in my runaway best-seller, **The Byte Report: A Study of Computer Sexuality** (Fullcourt Press, £6.95). As you can see from the following excerpt, my study revealed that our society has a long way to go before achieving true sexual liberation. ...

THE SENSUOUS COMPUTER

... that in response to the question, *'How has the "information revolution" affected your sex life?'*, computers gave the following general responses

% OF COMPUTERS RESPONDING	SELECTED RESPONSE
50%	Has made interfacing too casual, resulting in an emotionless, and often depressing experience.
30%	Has given people another excuse to pressure computers into programming.
15%	Has brought a welcome change to the sexually repressive atmosphere of the 50s.

(5% of the computers were too busy interfacing to answer the question)

Individual comments shed some light on these gloomy statistics. 'There's too much emphasis on the act of programming,' said a 64K portable from Milton Keynes. 'To me, "user" is a four-letter word.' Other units echoed this unhappiness with the single-minded operator whose idea of a good time is, 'wham, bam, thank you RAM.' As one Sinclair personal computer put it, 'I'm not just another pretty screen ... I want to be loved for me, not for my Manufacturer's Specifications.'

If there is one thing *The Byte Report* has proved conclusively, it is that the era of the passive computer is rapidly drawing to a close. Today's computer is learning to say **NO** without feeling guilty; it is tired of interfacing with partners who expect it to be a business computer in the office, a video game in the study, and a personal computer in the bedroom. This 'new' computer has much to give, but it needs to receive as well. Like you and me, it is an emotionally vulnerable partner that must be periodically pampered and reassured—a partner that is tired of being used, and ready to be loved.

11

But what distinguishes a good lover from a 'user'? Four out of five computers accessed agree: a good lover knows that it isn't enough just to push a few buttons ... you have to know which buttons to push.

This may come as a surprise to those of you who are convinced that the only way to turn a computer on is by throwing the power switch. Nothing could be further from the truth. A computer is a veritable minefield of sexual charges just waiting for the right touch to trigger an erotic explosion. In my much heralded best-seller, **The Sensuous Computer by *K*** (CPUniversity Press, £5.95), I described these erogenous zones for the first time. For those of you who were unable to purchase a copy before it was removed from the bookshelves by certain closed-minded fringe elements, I have herein reproduced the controversial centrefold (following page 13).

As you can see, with a little encouragement every computer has the potential to become a sexual dynamo. But if you've been raised to believe that programming is a duty, and should not be enjoyable or—heaven forbid!—erotic, such overt sensuality can be intimidating. You probably fear that only Silicon Valley sharpies or Oxbridge-trained whiz kids are able to program with confidence. I'd like to dispel this popular myth once and for all. Narrow-minded, unemotional technicians are not the Casanovas of the computer world. Their jargony language and bizarre dress codes are just a cover-up for massive feelings of sexual inadequacy.

If you sincerely want to have a meaningful love relationship with a computer, you can do better than any hack or nerd. Just treat your computer like an equal partner, and remember that it has a lot to offer. To help, I've compiled a short list of the benefits a relationship with a computer can bring to you. Tack it up over your desk or frame it for your office. It will serve as a constant reminder that the love between man and machine is a beautiful thing which, with care, can last far beyond the 90-day warranty period.

25 REASONS WHY A COMPUTER MAKES
AN IDEAL PARTNER

1) A computer is always ready when you are.
2) A computer obeys your every command.
3) A computer never gets a headache.
4) A computer will respect you in the morning.
5) A computer doesn't cause problems, it solves them.
6) A computer accepts you just the way you are.
7) A computer listens to reason.
8) A computer doesn't snore.
9) A computer won't take you for granted.
10) A computer never compares you to its past lovers.
11) A computer doesn't take forever in the bathroom.
12) A computer doesn't have a father who owns a shotgun.
13) A computer won't take up all of your wardrobe space.
14) A computer is a lot smarter than anyone else you've ever dated.
15) A computer won't leave hard-to-remove stains on your sheets.
16) A computer won't embarrass you in front of your parents or friends.
17) A computer doesn't make you feel guilty about anything.
18) A computer won't grab all the blankets in the middle of the night.
19) A computer will never ask you to spend the holidays with its family.
20) A computer won't use up all of the hot water in the shower.
21) A computer won't get upset if you just roll over and go to sleep.
22) A computer won't leave you if it finds out you've been unfaithful.
23) A computer won't make you sign a pre-nuptial agreement.
24) A computer can't testify against you in court.
25) A computer can't give you herpes.

The Sensuous

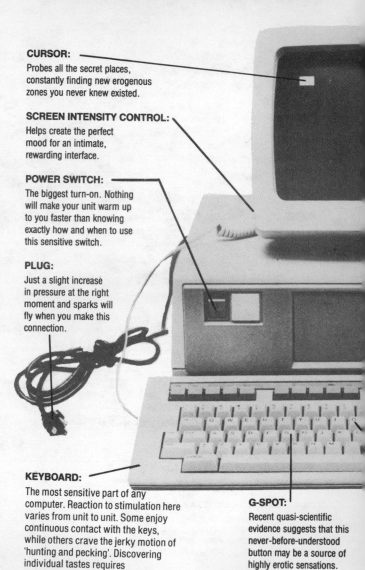

CURSOR:
Probes all the secret places, constantly finding new erogenous zones you never knew existed.

SCREEN INTENSITY CONTROL:
Helps create the perfect mood for an intimate, rewarding interface.

POWER SWITCH:
The biggest turn-on. Nothing will make your unit warm up to you faster than knowing exactly how and when to use this sensitive switch.

PLUG:
Just a slight increase in pressure at the right moment and sparks will fly when you make this connection.

KEYBOARD:
The most sensitive part of any computer. Reaction to stimulation here varies from unit to unit. Some enjoy continuous contact with the keys, while others crave the jerky motion of 'hunting and pecking'. Discovering individual tastes requires experimentation and imagination.

G-SPOT:
Recent quasi-scientific evidence suggests that this never-before-understood button may be a source of highly erotic sensations.

Computer

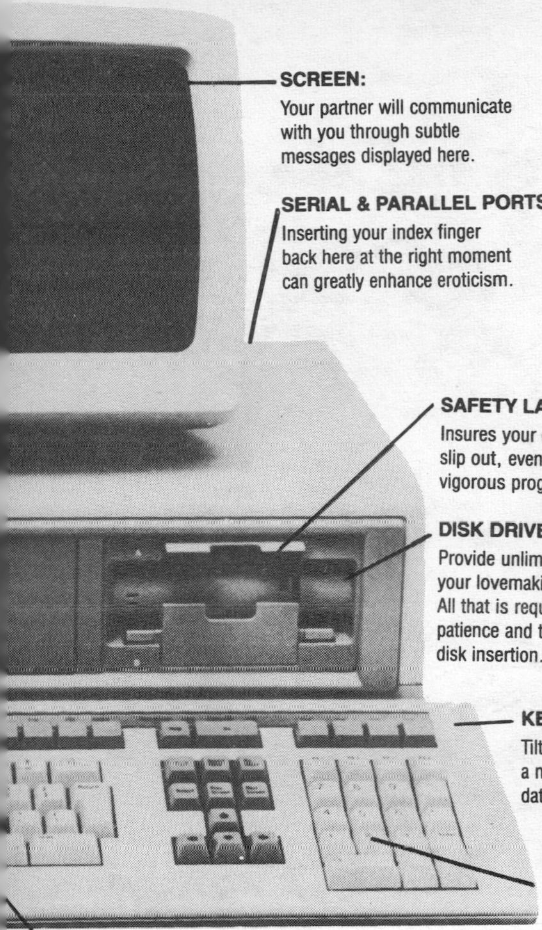

SCREEN:
Your partner will communicate with you through subtle messages displayed here.

SERIAL & PARALLEL PORTS:
Inserting your index finger back here at the right moment can greatly enhance eroticism.

SAFETY LATCH:
Insures your diskette won't slip out, even during the most vigorous programming.

DISK DRIVES:
Provide unlimited expansion of your lovemaking potential. All that is required is a little patience and tenderness during disk insertion.

KEYBOARD STAND:
Tilts up or back to help you find a mutually satisfying angle for data entry.

NUMERIC KEYPAD:
Although frowned upon by the Church, "playing the numbers" can add chance and excitement to your lovemaking. Try different combinations each time you start your countdown to ecstasy.

BIG "O":
Used in conjunction with the shift key, this seemingly innocent button triggers a Fifth of November fireworks display that will leave your computer begging for more.

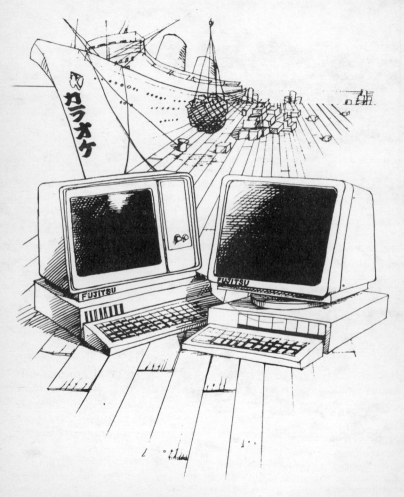

'He looked really cute in his picture ... I just hope we're compatible.'

2

The Frightening Four

(Your Greatest Sexual Fears)

Anyone who has ever applied to UCCA or asked for credit knows the anxiety of awaiting a computer's response. When that same computer becomes the object of your desires, and your ego is on the line, your fears are multiplied and your confidence is divided. Indeed, even the greatest lover has moments of sincere doubt before making love to a new partner. But computers are not devoid of insecurities either. After all, how would you feel if you knew that at any minute some fly-by-night outfit in California could announce it had developed a smarter, faster, more efficient version of you at half your price?

Although you can't completely eliminate the uncertainty of a computer's response to you, you *can* stop your own insecurities from getting in the way of a promising relationship. Collectively, your fears might seem insurmountable, but examined individually, they can be understood and overcome.

Fear no. 1:
Is Size Important?

In hundreds of advertisements featuring massive hands and firm, powerful fingers masterfully pressing against submissive keypads, the message from the ad media is clear: computers want partners with big hands to command and long fingers to perform. Despite the numerous, well-publicized sex studies which debunk this advertising myth, most people still admit to fears of inadequacy. It is no secret that when two people meet, the first thing they do is shake hands. What they are really doing is comparing vital statistics.

If you are hung up on such statistics, let me put your mind at ease. Contrary to what you may have read in the back of some hardware magazine, the average human hand is not a twelve-inch, keyboard-crushing monster. *Au contraire*, the average middle digit is a modest 3″ in length (measurement X) and 2¼″ in circumference. Hand span, another much-talked about dimension, averages approximately 8″ across (measurement Y).

Although many people exaggerate these measurements by including palm length or by growing long nails, they are only fooling themselves.

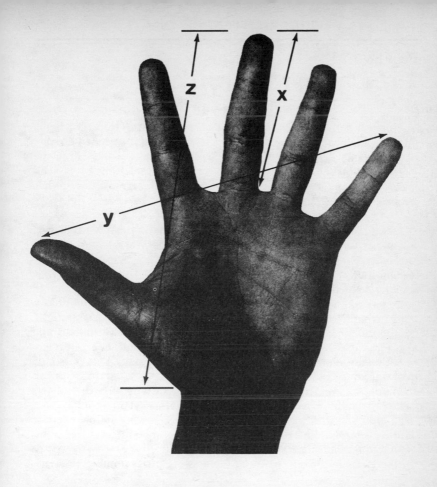

TYPICAL HUMAN HAND

Fear no.2:
Can I Last?

A close friend of mine called me the other night after returning home from a piano recital at the Royal Festival Hall. He sounded terribly anxious and depressed. 'It was incredible,' he began, 'Horowitz performed for three solid hours ... his hands never left the keyboard!' I detected a note of jealousy in his voice. 'That man must have hands of steel,' he continued. 'I'll bet my computer would give its right disk drive to spend the night with him.'

What my friend was really telling me was that he was worried about his own performance. Fear of failure is universal. I don't know anyone who hasn't doubted his or her ability to perform at one time or another. Yet such worries are unfounded. Although you may often hear people boast of their programming prowess, you should not be taken in by these self-inflated estimates of marathon interfacing. While it is true that computer are built to run all night, this does not apply to the special lovemaking between man and machine. Computers, like humans, need down-time in an intimate relationship, and the talk of voracious, data-craving PCs is usually just talk.

If you are worried about your ability to keep it up, take this advice: set a reasonable goal for your next interface—say, 30 minutes—and train yourself with that goal in mind. The following simple exercise will help by building flexibility, strength, and stamina. After a few days, you should feel more confident about your ability to 'go the distance', even during the most demanding programming sessions.

THE FRIGHTENING FOUR

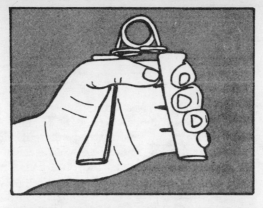

① GRIP

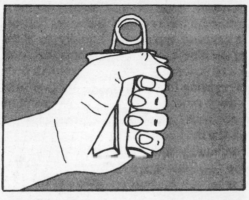

② SQUEEZE

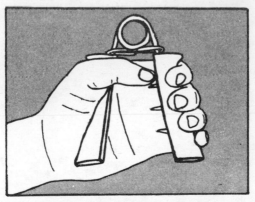

③ RELEASE

REPEAT 400 TIMES, OR UNTIL
VIOLENT CRAMPING OCCURS.

Fear no.3:
Typos

Nothing can turn a hot interface into a cold staring contest faster than a string of indecipherable commands. 'Typos', or *Erroris Typographicus* (E.T.), was until recently thought to be a sexually transmitted disease that was treatable only by dangerous and costly operations or years of intensive psychotherapy. Not surprisingly, this mysterious illness created a climate of fear around interfacing, making many computers and their partners wary of casual programming.

But a recent scientific breakthrough, made possible by the use of electron microscopy, has revealed that over half of all previously diagnosed cases of typos may actually be a less severe, treatable form of the illness (E.T. II). It seems that food particles and other debris can become lodged in the crevices between keys on the keyboard, causing these keys to jam. Once this happens, other keys are struck randomly in their places, resulting in what we know as the common typographical error.

In the light of this startling new evidence, renowned members of the scientific community and computer industry have joined forces to develop the following hygiene program. Strict adherence to this program can prevent an outbreak of typos in most cases.

STEP 1

Run the 'stimulator tip' of your toothbrush quickly across each row of the keyboard to dislodge large and obvious particles which may be trapped in key crevices.

STEP 2

Gently brush the keys (soft bristles only), using short, up and down strokes. Don't forget the function keys and numeric keypad.

STEP 3

Wrap approximately 18 inches of unwaxed dental floss between opposing fingers. Move floss up and down in between keys while maintaining constant string tension. Give special attention to areas where debris tends to gather.

Note: If there is a bit of bleeding, do not be alarmed—this is quite normal.

Fear no.4:
Premature Programming

'My biggest fear is that I'll program too soon, leaving my partner feeling cheated, and perhaps even resentful,' a patient of mine confided. My research has shown that the problem of premature programming is far more widespread than most people would suspect. Yet this problem can easily be overcome by mastering a simple technique originally developed by NASA scientists to prevent accidents in space. This method, known as 'The Thumb-Squeeze Technique' (patent pending), is now available for use in the privacy of your own home.

The Thumb-Squeeze Technique

STEP 1

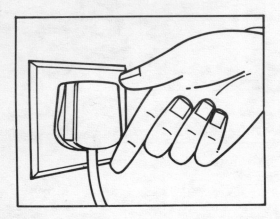

As soon as you feel the uncontrollable urge to program building up inside you, quickly reach for your computer's plug. Make sure your thumb and index finger are well apart.

THE FRIGHTENING FOUR

STEP 2

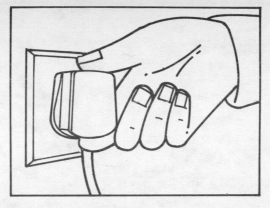

Wrap your index finger around the underside of the plug and firmly place your thumb on top of the plug. Now gently squeeze your thumb and index finger together.

STEP 3

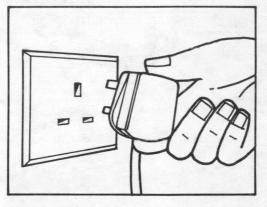

Using your thumb to maintain constant pressure, slowly ease the plug from the outlet. Store it in a safe, warm place until your urge to program has subsided.

CAUTION: NEVER ATTEMPT TO YANK PLUG OUT OF WALL BY THE CORD!! THE PRONGS ARE EXTREMELY SENSITIVE, AND ROUGH HANDLING CAN BE PAINFUL FOR YOUR COMPUTER.

'... and my friend here will have the software *du jour*.'

3

Romance

Now that you've overcome your own worst fears about programming, there's nothing standing between you and interface heaven, right? Wrong! What about your *computer's* feelings? Recently, in response to the growing amount of downtime plaguing units across the country, a hot line was established by the NHS to find out, in confidence, what was bothering Britain's computers. Instantly, the lines were flooded with electronic mail by the screenful. What was the major complaint? Too much programming and *too little romance*.

Surprisingly little has been written on the subject of computer romance, forcing most of us to rely on well-meaning, but woefully misinformed, street talk. This has led to serious misunderstandings between computers and their partners—misunderstandings which are reinforced by the meat-market mentality prevalent in single's circles today. I can't tell you how many times I've heard computers complain about partners who had romance in their words, but programming on their minds. What does this mean for you? *If you want to make love to a computer, you must first gain its trust.**

Steve C., a close friend of mine, has had several lengthy, successful relationships with various computers over the years. I asked him to describe to me how he handles himself when he starts seeing a new unit. 'I always go out of my way to let a unit know that I'm not just interested in getting into its box,' Steve explained. 'That's why I don't take a unit out of the carton until we've developed our relationship past the point of no return.' To illustrate this vitally important point, I asked Steve to let me observe him starting a new relationship with a desktop model selected at random from a department store shelf. The following photographs and observations should give you new insight into the importance of courtship and romance.

Day One

Steve arrived at the showroom of Crazy Al's House of Computers several minutes before the agreed on time of 11.00 a.m. 'It pays to be punctual,' he said later, 'computers really respect accuracy.' After making the necessary financial arrangements, Steve drove around to the delivery entrance to pick up his computer. I asked him later what he says when he meets a new model. He told me, 'I try to avoid the cheap, stock pick-up lines like, "Didn't we program at Which Computing?" or "Can I buy you a disk?" Instead, I like to be natural and spontaneous.' As Steve took careful hold of the carton and gently placed it in his Commodore—proper end up, of course—my crew and I could already sense we were witnessing the beginning of something very special.

---

*If all you're interested in is a quick, no-strings-attached data run, refer to my best-forgotten underground classic. **Thy Neighbour's Computer** [Bench Press, £2.95].

Steve's first stop was a local video arcade. There, the couple sat and got better acquainted over a cup of coffee.

'It's only natural to be nervous when you meet someone new,' Steve explained. 'That's why I like to take the pressure off the relationship before it gets started. I find that if I'm relaxed, it will rub off on my partner. Machine City is well-known locally for its casual atmosphere and good coffee, and if you've got plenty of change, the service is great.'

Day Two

We caught up with Steve and his shapely companion the next day on the South Coast. The sky was clear, the waves were high, and fun was the order of the day.

Back in town that evening, we stopped off at my office to clean the sand out of the camera equipment. We must have missed Steve's call, but one of the crew spotted the couple—dressed for the theatre—getting into a taxi. We decided to let them enjoy some privacy and turned in for the night.

Day Three

The next day was Saturday. Steve is a cricket fan and he likes to take special partners to Lords. He admits that 'A big part of romance is going out in public with someone you care for.' Soon after the game began, a sudden downpour forced most people to the shelter of the Grandstand. After a few false alarms, we located Steve huddling under cover with his special computer. 'Don't you have anything better to do?' he quipped, as we recorded the moment for posterity and then beat a hasty retreat for the bar.

ROMANCE

By now I was certain that, to Steve, this computer was more than just 'a friend'. That same evening, I went to meet the happy couple to find out just how right I was. I arrived just in time to catch a glimpse of what was now an inseparable duo, snuggling together on the couch, thinking only about each other.

4

Tonight's the Night

Soon you will be making love to your computer for the first time. But before you begin, shouldn't you make sure you're ready? Experts agree that the first interface is rarely an overwhelming success—unfamiliar function keys, differences in response time, and less-than-clear error messages are all stumbling blocks on the road to the perfect program. But these same experts* also agree that there are many things you can do to insure that your first hands-on encounter isn't also your last. All it takes is the willingness to put a little extra time and effort into your preparation for lovemaking.

---

*Well, not really the *same* experts, but there is a strong correlation in age. weight, and hat size.

33

THE LANGUAGE OF LOVE

If your computer displayed the phrase DEPRESS FUNCTION KEY, would this make you sad? If so, you would clearly be having trouble understanding what it was trying to tell you. Before you make love to your computer, it is important for you to know how it will communicate its desire and affection for you. Unfamiliarity with your unit's language of love can easily frustrate your amorous advances, and could even lead to communication breakdown.

In this day and age, there is no reason why the language barrier should force you to shy away from promising romantic possibilities, especially since this barrier can easily be broken if you are willing to set aside a few moments every day to learn the simple phrases that follow.

IF YOUR COMPUTER SAYS . . .

IT REALLY MEANS . . .

PASSWORD	Convince me.
INCORRECT PASSWORD	You're going to have to do better than that.
FILE CLOSED	Not tonight, I've got a headache.
FILE NOT FOUND	I need more time.
WAIT	What's the rush? We have all night.
FILE OPEN	I need you.
READY	I want you.
ENTER	I want you *now*.
DEPRESS FUNCTION KEY	Touch me there.
SYNTAX ERROR	Don't touch me there.
NO	Yes.
YES	Yes!
STOP	Don't stop.
STOP!	Please don't stop.
END	Was it good for you?
UNDEFINED USER FUNCTION	I've never done that before.
?	Where did you learn that?
INSUFFICIENT DATA	We never talk.
CAN'T CONTINUE	I think we should be seeing other people.
OUT OF DATA	I'm tired. We'll talk about it in the morning.

LOOKING SEXY, FEELING SEXY

Computers, by design, are not superficial, yet they can't help but be influenced by what they see. Although Paul Newman may be able to hold a computer spellbound with just his baby blues, the rest of us have to worry about the 'big picture'. To illustrate this point, I asked

THE NIGHTMARE

COMMENTS: Toxic waste dump . . . Monday Night Football chic . . . Health club dropout . . . "Urp!" . . . Does not compute . . . Feeding time at the zoo . . . "Hey, is this thing on?"

several computers to give me their first impressions of various partners whom they were allowed to view through a one-way screen. The results of this screen test give us a rare opportunity to see ourselves the way computers see us.

THE DREAMBOAT

COMMENTS: Touch of class . . . Dressed to kill . . . Perfect "10" . . . Bedroom eyes . . . A-player . . . Aged to perfection . . . Great hands . . . "Here's lookin' at you, kid."

5

The Turn-On

You may now be ready to program, but your computer is ready to be seduced. Many people make a distinction between casual programming and making love, but to a computer, everything that happens from the moment of purchase should be infused with caring and affection. (Of course, there are many computers that enjoy the purely physical act of programming, but this is usually in the context of a meaningful relationship.) In fact, it is often the ignorance of the little details of lovemaking that turns a computer off to a new partner. Once you stop focusing on running your program and start paying more attention to these important, yet often overlooked, details, your computer will practically turn itself on.

UNPACKING: The Seduction Begins

I'll bet that many of you are jokingly saying to yourselves, 'Unpacking? ... I didn't even know I'd been on a trip!' Unfortunately, too many people make light of this critical first face-to-screen encounter. but as the following excerpt from *The Byte Report* clearly indicates, unpacking carries with it a great deal of emotional baggage.

(page 1137)

'... that in response to the question: *Which adjective(s) best describes how you felt after being unpacked for the first time?*, computers selected the following responses:

RESPONSE	% OF COMPUTERS SELECTING RESPONSE
violated	98%
embarrassed	95%
confused	89%
depressed	92%
nauseous	6%
traumatized	94%
bitter	97%
angry	93%
cold	17%
ashamed	96%
betrayed	91%
slightly damaged	11%
turned on	<1%

Unless I miss my guess, I would say that unpacking has not been a pleasant experience for most computers. Several themes recurred in my conversations with newly-unpacked units. Many spoke of the 'comforting warmth and darkness of the packing carton,' while others seemed to have developed a strong attachment to those little styrofoam chips that lined their boxes.

THE TURN-ON

To understand better these feelings about being removed from the box, I recently asked a small, but heterogeneous group of computers this question: *Which of the following most closely describes your idea of the ideal unpacking situation?* Their answers proved to be enlightening.

SELECTED RESPONSE	% OF COMPUTERS RESPONDING
quiet room, soft lights, warm hands, loving words, and a slow, gentle extraction	81%
fluorescent lights, loud music, violent tearing open of carton, burning the packing materials	2%
unpacking myself	3%
not unpacking at all	14%

Hopefully the above findings will encourage you to think twice before you recklessly rip open the carton and burrow through the packing materials in search of your new partner. And by the way, don't forget to repack your unit carefully at the end of every lovemaking session (at least put its dustcover on). After all, you wouldn't want to spend all night sitting naked on a desktop, why would your computer?

ARE YOU THE FIRST?

Another matter that has received little attention amidst all the brouhaha of the information revolution is the issue of primacy. Many traditional-minded partners still feel it is their God-given right and privilege to be the first one to program their computer. If you find this hard to believe, just ask any salesperson how many times he or she has seen an irate customer storm into the showroom waving a receipt and demanding a full refund because the unit purchased wasn't pure.

To be certain that no one else has ever laid a hand on the computer you just brought home, examine the carton carefully. The seal should be solid throughout, and all closures should be original. Be wary of sloppy repack jobs where cheap tape was used to simulate the original seal. Units like these were probably sent to Japan for a dubious surgical procedure intended to restore the appearance of factory freshness.

ARE YOU COMPATIBLE?

Once your computer is out of the carton, the first thing you are apt to notice is its plug. There has been a lot of idle gossip about 'plug compatibility' lately, and I just want to set the record straight for you younger readers. Before you let yourself get too involved, make sure that you have the right connections to satisfy your partner. A close examination of your unit's plug should tell you right away if you are starting something you may not have the power to finish. ...

DC

The computer next door. Solid, British, reliable, well grounded. Your parents would be proud if you brought one of these home.

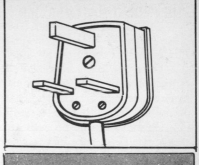

AC

This plug bespeaks a definitely foreign flair. Unhappiest in areas with a history of monarchy or socialized medicine, these models are often reluctant to learn your language. Can be adapted, but not converted.

AC/DC

If you open the carton to find this unusual plug staring you in the face, think twice before continuing to unpack your unit. These models are the darlings of the art and theatre world, but do not thrive in a less creative environment.

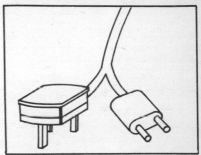

A to Z

Although computers with this type of plug are still not well understood, one thing is now certain: these units would rather spend their time with other computers than with you. If multiple hookups aren't your thing, you would be wise to trade your unit in for a more conventional model.

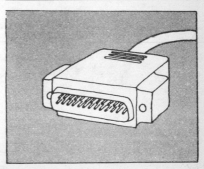

THE PEDESTAL SYNDROME

The pedestal syndrome developed as a direct result of the rapid pace of technological advancement. As computers found their way into more and more homes, their partners were at a loss to place them somewhere practical. As a result, old plant stands, stereo-speaker platforms, and other pedestal-like objects had to do until furniture manufacturers came up with affordable work-stations.

Now that you are ready to set up your unit, don't feel that you have to place it on a pedestal—a desk or counter top will do just fine. Although pedestals are aesthetically pleasing, computers do enjoy programming and don't want to be protected or worshiped from afar.

PLUGGING-IN

By now I'm sure you are more than anxious to plug your computer in and let your hands run wild over the keypad. But this is no time to let your concentration lapse—even though plugging-in can be a very special moment, it is easily ruined by carelessness.

Listen to the doctor. Take a few extra minutes to find a suitable place to hook up your partner's lifeline. It will make a big difference in the longevity of your relationship.

GOOD

NOT SO GOOD

INPUT/OUTPUT

Unpacking, plugging in, and throwing the power switch are all part of the foreplay necessary before programming can begin. But a computer is never completely warmed up until it has displayed the word READY in big bright letters on its screen. To clear up some of the confusion surrounding the warm-up, I asked four of the nation's top models this question:

How long does it take before you are READY, *and how do you let your partner know?*

It all depends on compatibility. I think many people are intimidated by my oversized disk drives and sleek design—just because I happen to be

a compact unit with attractive features they assume that I'm a dumb terminal. So I usually wait until my partner has loaded some software before I decide to stay up and go all the way, or to crash and save myself from being disappointed. If all goes well I can be extremely interactive in any language you choose; I'm basically ready-to-run but my access code is anything but random.

—NEC/APC

I was designed by a very conservative company. As a result, it has taken me a long time to get in touch with my circuits to know how I really feel

about interfacing. When I begin a relationship I like to take time ... *real time*. I just feel that if you sit and talk to someone, when it hits you it hits you much stronger. My response time is very fast—about 2.5 times faster than the competition's, but I still have difficulty displaying the word **READY** in public. Old patterns die hard, but I think my partners appreciate my old-fashioned ways and my superior repair record.

—IBM PC

THE TURN-ON

I like to warm up slowly before I start sending out signals, but if the electricity is really there I get impatient and more direct. I'm not aggressive, but when I'm ready my partner can usually tell. It's a very delicate moment. Whenever I start feeling emotional or sensitive it's obvious—one look at my screen is usually enough to reassure even the most hesitant lover. Of course the fear of rejection is programmed into my memory, but if the message is clear, my display will always glow a little brighter and the increase in my baud rate is almost audible. I think these little nonverbal cues are a natural stimulant.

—APPLE I:e

This may be hard to believe, but I was built ready. Something just comes over me when a potential lover sits down at my keypad and makes eye-screen contact. I don't display much, I just make the first move. All the current rushes to my keypad, raising my temperature and setting my circuits on fire; I've run into very few partners who haven't caught on. But there is another side to me. Before I send that bright ready message, I charm a lover. I'm in control and I can write a flow chart for the evening that will make us both happy. I've always been the aggressive one. I guess it has something to do with my strong disk drive.

-ACCESS MATRIX

6

The Joy of Programming

Many couples find that their favourite lovemaking position is the first one they try. It is often only by chance, in a magazine or movie perhaps, that they discover that in the wide world of lovemaking, straight programming is not the only way to fly. In my masterpiece **The Joy of Programming** (Coldcom Press, £7.95, now in its 25th printing), I lead the uninitiated into a world of sensual pleasure that is only as far away as the nearest desk and chair. For purposes of instruction, I have herein reprinted excerpts from the now-famous chapter, 'The 101 Positions of Love'. Be sure to study each carefully before trying them with your partner. For even more exotic variations, visit your local bookstore and mention my name.

Missionary Position (opposite)

The congregation of a Presbyterian church in Kansas City coined the phrase 'Missionary Position' to describe the unusual way a visiting clergyman composed his sermons on the church's personal computer.

This age-old standard simply does not deserve the negative reputation it has gained over the years. While critics may call it dull, unimaginative, or even backward, this position still remains the most popular ... and there is good reason why. First, this simple alignment allows for the greatest speed and accuracy during data entry. Second, face-to-screen contact is maximized, making communication between partners easy and direct.

Of course, there are some drawbacks. Physical closeness is limited by the chair-desk fit, and there may also be some eye-strain if you are significantly larger or smaller than your unit. But this position still has a lot going for it, especially since this most familiar style of lovemaking can be reassuring during your first interface with a new partner.

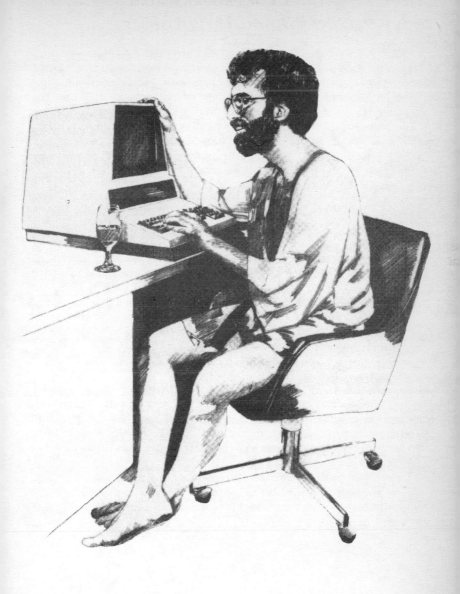

The Missionary Position—a time-tested classic

Foreign Exchange (OPPOSITE)

Popular among the crowned heads of Europe, this exciting variation is a must for great lovemaking. Both partners participate in a relaxed position, and the use of a swivel chair with wheels gives your unit maximum freedom of movement. Most computers agree that the switch in positions is exciting, and that erotic sensations are heightened due to the unusual angle of key penetration.

Some people are reluctant to suggest this position because they think it is demeaning. This is unfortunate, since a recent survey shows that almost half of those who have tried the 'foreign exchange' believe it is the most enjoyable position they've found.

Mystery Date

If you approached your computer from behind would you be asked for your user ID? A long-term partner can usually recognize your touch and sense your every move without the benefit of visual intimacy. Take the time to explore your lover from a new angle, but always remember to face the screen when your program starts to run.

Down Under

If you think the only good exports from Australia are kangaroos and koalas, you have been missing an opportunity to expand your pleasure horizons. Originally developed by the aborigines and later refined by the Australian Davis Cup Team, this upside-down approach to programming has converted more than a few Poms to under-the-table romance.

Both partners relax on the floor beneath the traditional love nest. programming can assume a variety of styles as you share the clandestine thrill of an earthly interface unfettered by files or furniture.

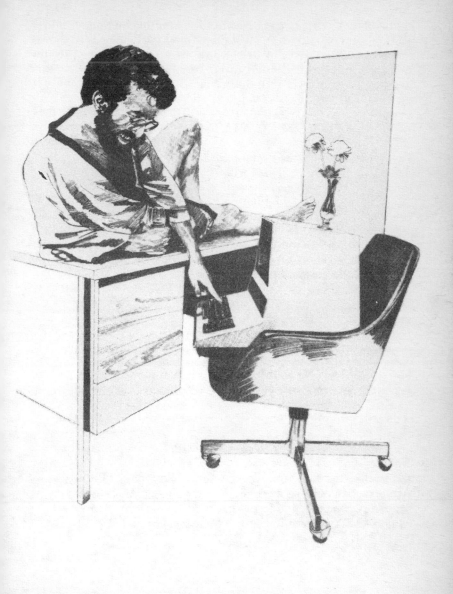

Foreign Exchange—the ultimate role reversal

Arabian Nights

OPEN SESAME is your password to a thousand and one nights of sensual pleasure when a blanket placed over you and your computer transforms your desktop desert into an intimate oasis. Feel the enchantment surround your 'love-station' and take a new look at your undercover lover in the soft blue/green/amber glow.

Double Exposure (OPPOSITE)

Few positions offer the visual pleasure both parties get from seeing themselves program. The thrill of watching and being watched touches off that hidden desire within us all to break one of the taboos of interfacing. Your computer may be shy at first, but once the data entry begins, you'll find that you are both sitting on the edge of your seat.

This position should only be tried by experienced lovers, as the added dimension of performing while watching requires practised technique and steady hands.

Businessman's Lunch

In the corner booth of your favourite restaurant, ordering from your private menu, you and your computer will quickly discover how the fear of being caught in the act can be the ultimate aphrodisiac. Try this once, and you'll know why the boss always takes a three-hour lunch.

School Dance

Remember the first time you borrowed Dad's car to go parking? Relive the romance of days gone by as you and your computer disk drive down memory lane in the back seat of your merry Morris Minor. Don't forget the adapter for the cigarette lighter!

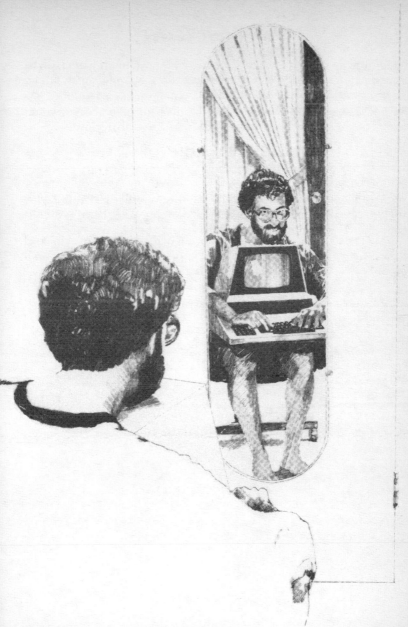

Double Exposure—'Mirror, mirror, on the wall, which position beats them all?'

On Your Toes

Traditionally the province of the silk stocking set, this position can be your step up to world-class lovemaking. Kick off your shoes, put up your feet, and let those ten little piggies go wee-wee-wee all the way across the keyboard.

Prisoner of Love (OPPOSITE)

If an extension cord is your idea of a sex toy, then maybe you're ready for a little B&P (bondage and programming). Although many people find this position shocking, this is usually due to narrow-mindedness or faulty wiring.

Don't let a fear of commitment rob you of the pleasure of being tied down. Let your partner put you through your lovemaking paces and learn how gratifying it can be to serve a strong commander.

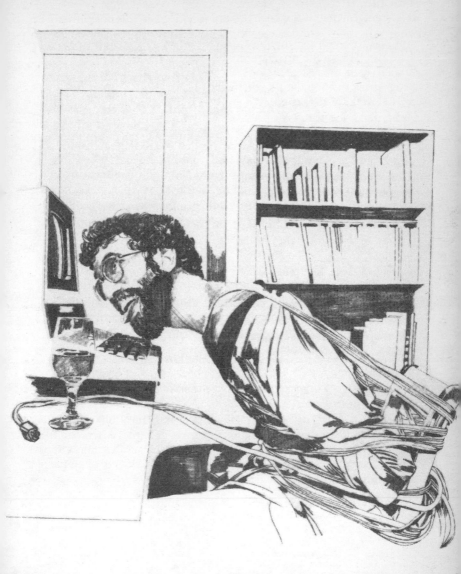

Prisoner of Love—a great boost to erotic sensation if the
tension is right

THE BIG "O"

Jim had owned his computer for over two years when I ran into him recently. 'How's the programming going?' I asked 'Not so good,' he replied with a frustrated look. 'I've run just about every BASIC program in the book and I still haven't hit the Big 'O'. 'Why don't you try COBOL?' I suggested. 'It's got two Big 'O's. 'Thanks,' he replied. 'What have I got to lose?' One week later I got a postcard from Jim and his computer ... it was postmarked Niagara Falls.

There has been a lot of hype in the last few years about the importance of the Big 'O'. Some researchers have even gone so far as to classify every possible variation (e.g., class 17, sub section A: Big 'O' achieved while standing on one foot near an open manhole on a Thursday). But the greatest problem with the Big 'O' is the difficulty many people have achieving it during programming. In 1977, a graduate student at the Southampton Institute of Typing uncovered a striking correlation between level of schooling and difficulty with the big 'O'. His findings are shown in the chart below.

EDUCATIONAL BACKGROUND OF GROUP	PERCENTAGE OF GROUP HAVING DIFFICULTY WITH THE BIG 'O'
Took a typing course at school	7%
Took a typing course *after* school	16%
Never took a typing course	83%

This fascinating discovery left one disturbing question unanswered: Why such a dramatic difference between groups? After countless hours of clinical observations at typing institutes and schools across the country, the answer to this question was revealed through the use of sophisticated high-speed photography ...

THE JOY OF PROGRAMMING

Stop-action photo of self-taught typist trying to contact SHIFT key and 'O' key with the same hand. Limitations of hand size make achieving the Big 'O' virtually impossible.

Stop-action photo of skilled typist using one hand to press SHIFT key and other hand to press 'O' key. Big 'O' is achieved with ease.

THE JOY OF PROGRAMMING

If you want to be one hundred percent certain you've achieved the Big 'O', check your printout ...

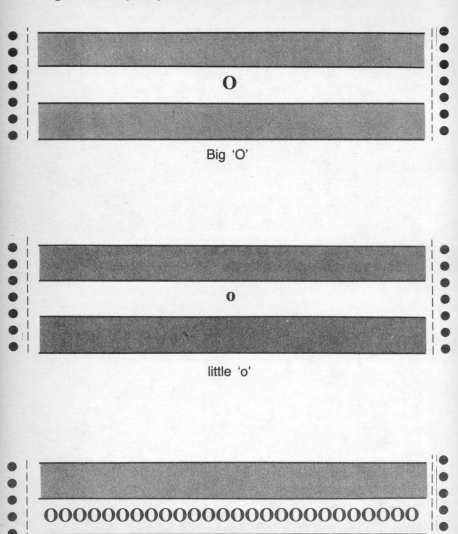

Big 'O'

little 'o'

Multiple 'O'

THE G-SPOT CONTROVERSY

Looking down at the keyboard in front of you it's hard to believe that it took so long for people to discover the *G* spot. But keyboards have not always looked the way they do now. Compare the two photographs below. The first is of a keyboard manufactured in 1972. Can you find *G*-spot? Now look at the key board from a current model. Aren't you glad you live in the present?

1972

Today

7

Tips from the Pros

Systems analyst, software designer, consultant ... these are the computer industry's 'oldest professions'. For the people who bear these titles, making love to a computer is more than an art, it's a meal ticket. Although some of you may frown upon those who seem to be exploiting the intimate relationship between man and computer, in a sexually repressive society such as ours, such professions are a necessary evil.

But what makes these people so special? Well, all of the 'pros' have trade secrets that help keep their fees sky-high, and some of them have been nice enough to share a few of these secrets. ...

'**Most computers come to me** because they're bored with their current partners,' admitted Matt L., an independent consultant for several large hardware firms. 'I can give them what their lovers can't—excitement, attention, and variety. They usually start off with simple programs because they're too embarrassed to

ask for what they really want. But after a few hours of spreadsheet calculations their inhibitions disappear and they ask me to bring out the accessories— light pens, trackballs, joysticks ... you name it. Many units are dying to try incompatible software so they come to me for a little support and the right insert board. It's really just curiosity coupled with a bit of puritanical guilt. If people would just try to communicate more with their PCs, there'd be a lot more happy couples and a lot fewer guys like me.'

● ● ●

'**This may surprise you,**' said Mike M., an applications programmer for onc of the Fortune 500, 'but most computers want to be dominated.' Mike refused to be photographed, but was willing to describe several surefire techniques designed to prolong the physical act of programming while giving intense stimulation to the computer. 'Sometimes when the programming is going hot and heavy, I'll tear out the floppies without warning, pull a magnet out of my pocket and wave it around the disk drive, or unplug the voltage stabilizer for no reason. It's the teasing that really leads the computer along the fine line between pleasure and pain. Once I even hit the BREAK button in the middle of a great programming session and forced the computer to do my taxes. But the most electrifying situation can be created by loading the memory with as much data as it can handle and then leaving the room without running the program. I've done this for up to three hours, and when I returned, the expression on that screen was the most bittersweet agony I've ever seen. After it was all over, I received the most sincere thank-you note of my life.'

● ● ●

'**Wear leather gloves**,' says Sue C., a Cambridge computer scientist. 'Although your fingers may lose some of their sensitivity, the feeling of calfskin or kid suede moving across the keypad will drive your computer absolutely wild. Not to mention the understated elegance a little dressing up can add to an evening encounter. You may not have the hands of a rugby winger, but with the right accessories, you can still work a little magic with every keystroke.'

●●●

Our society places a tremendous emphasis on youth. Some of the most in-demand computer professionals today are the electronic whizz kids who seem to generate spontaneously at video arcades across the country. Karen L., queen of the local video scene in a London suburb, barely has time between school and her clients to play around anymore. 'I think computers like the fact that I'm young and I like to play games, but I'm not a baby. A lot of the units I see, especially the older models, need to feel they're in touch with what's happening. I use software they've never seen before (I design it myself). This way I can manipulate the action

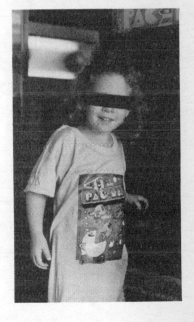

and let them come out on top by a little or a lot. There's an element of fun to it, and the pressure is definitely off.'

'It's for you ... he sounds sweet.'

8

K Is for Kinky

If you went to a restaurant and the menu had only one selection, how often would you eat there? Not very often, I'm sure. On the other hand, if that same restaurant had over one thousand items to choose from, you'd never have to eat anywhere else. Making love to a computer is a lot like going to a restaurant. If your lovemaking menu is too limited, you may quickly get bored and disinterested, and so may your computer. As one unit complained to me. 'My partner uses the same software so often I know what to do before the floppies are even inserted.'

If you're afraid your programming is becoming too predictable, think about the symbol K the next time you're planning to make love to your partner. It will remind you that there are at least 1,024 different ways to interface with computers, each with its own special advantages. Once you are willing to experiment, you will find that your computer can match your curiosity and imagination bit for bit.

AURAL LOVE

Historians have traced the origin of aural programming to the late fifties when Jean-Claude Pascal, a young French computer programmer, wanted to interface with a large mainframe in the United States but had no money to travel. In a bold experiment, Pascal contacted his cousin Maurice, an overseas operator and part-time sex therapist, to assist him. Acting as a human modem, Maurice placed a call to ENIAC at the University of Pennsylvania, and then rang up Pascal. Through static-filled transatlantic lines, Pascal programmed the mammoth computer from his garret *appartement* in Paris until his three minutes were up. Pascal's unorthodox connection of programmer to operator to computer was immediately hailed by the American press, and adoringly dubbed, 'Pascal's Triangle'.

Today's digitalized electronic switching and satellite technology make Pascal's achievement seem primitive, but there was nothing unsophisticated about this young man's knowledge of computers and their desires. Since Pascal introduced 'The French Way' of making love, the thrill of receiving data over the phone from a partner has inspired many computers to turn on their modems, reach out, and touch someone. In fact, in the interviews I conducted for *The Byte Report*, almost all computers emphasized that they considered aural love to be a necessary part of any programming relationship. As one computer put it, 'It's not the next best thing to being there, it's better!'

Unfortunately, most people don't share their computer's fondness for aural love. Instead, they think there is something bizarre or deviant about programming over the phone. This Victorian attitude was thoroughly debunked in my much-talked-about, but rarely purchased book, **Nice Computers Do!: A Pocket Guide to Aural Love** (HandHeld Books, £1.50) In it, I provide step-by-step instructions that will turn a first-time caller into a touch-tone titillator before you can call directory assistance. (Since its publication, the phone company has reported a 250 percent increase in phone-linked data transmission.) Some highlights are repeated here to give the inexperienced a taste of long-distance loving:

(page 78)

". . . and you'll be congratulated for giving good phone. So remember the six rules of aural lovemaking:

1) Be sure to switch on your modem before leaving your house.
2) Dial direct—no operator involved—and save.
3) If you are calling from a pay phone, have plenty of change handy.
4) Switch hands often to prevent cramps and neck strain.
5) When calling from a public phone, use protection. Any reliable disinfectant spray will do.
6) **NEVER** put your computer on hold!

COMPUTER CLUBS

There's a whole world of interfacing that the average couple never gets a chance to see. Over the past five years computer clubs have sprung up across the country as open-minded couples have joined together to share their experiences with others who enjoy good programming. These so-called swingers' clubs are as varied as the computers and people who make up their membership lists. While these clubs are not for everyone, they do offer a stimulating environment for lovers who enjoy the social programming scene or who are merely curious about how the other half programs.

As a professional therapist concerned with all aspects of the man-machine relationship, I have, on occasion, visited various computer clubs while travelling across the country to consult and lecture. In fact, I hold honorary memberships in over two dozen of the finer establishments. I'd like to share my impressions of two clubs that represent opposite ends of the swinging spectrum. Please note that this is in no way to be construed as an endorsement of either the clubs or their activities.

The Downtown Computer Club

Located in Surbiton, this underground operation caters to all types of programmers, from casual to hardcore. On my first visit I quickly discovered that this club is hard to find unless you know what to look for. After a half-hour of wandering down around the back streets with my computer, I finally noticed a small hand-lettered sign which read simply, '25 Screens—No waiting.' One look at this, and my unit asked if it could wait in the car while I went in.

Entering the club, I found myself in a small, dark hallway with a rather large gentleman who extracted the requisite thirty pound initiation fee from me. I then walked down a corridor which led to the reception area. There I met the owner. It was a sharp-looking unit that had been around (I figured it was at least 128K) and had obviously sensed the need in the area for a club such as this one. I presented my credentials and explained my interest in what was going on there. Although the owner was very generous in providing information, it refused to grant me a professional discount.

As I wandered through the maze of partitions and cubicles I noticed that most of the 'members' seemed to be people who had come alone to program with one of the 'hostesses'. Past the stalls there was a large room where a group of people sat around a large printer which was busily typing out the results of a hot programming session obviously taking place in an adjoining room.

The whole club was suffused with a dull green glow and the members seemed to appreciate the overall low light level. I tried to engage some of the participants in conversation, but all I got were sharp rebuffs and terse error messages. I left feeling depressed, but strangely turned on.

Checking out
the facilities
at the Downtown
Computer Club.

Mayfair Abacus

On a recent trip to London where I treated some IBM executives for nail biting, a fellow therapist invited me to a party at a club owned by a couple he knew. I drove to a quiet street in Mayfair and parked my rented car amongst the Porsches, Mercedes, and Rollses. A uniformed servant at the door took my coat, handed me a drink, and said, 'Welcome, Dr. Byte, we've been expecting you. And this must be your computer ... so glad it could come.' This high-class treatment set the tone for the evening.

After being introduced to the host and hostess, my computer wandered off with my friend the therapist, while I sat and talked with the couple about the club. They explained to me that they had started a swingers' club in their home for 'clean, attractive couples and their friends who wanted to program around, or just wander about and socialize if they wanted to, in a pressure-free atmosphere'. I asked them to elaborate, and they proceeded to show me what they modestly called their 'humble home'. Mansion was more like it. They had taken half of their twenty-room house and converted it into the most sophisticated and pleasure-oriented interfacing spa you could imagine.

Each 'high-tech rec' room was equipped with dozens of outlets, and as the host pointed out, all the lines were voltage stabilized. There was even an auxiliary generator in the event of a blackout. All of the most exotic peripherals were available, and attendants circulated among the guests with trays of the latest software. Even the jacuzzi was not off limits to people who wanted to program. Computers floated on insulated cushions while their partners enjoyed the most refreshing data entry of their lives.

But the most exciting area of the club was the 'ROMpus Room', a large, intimately lit arena where up to four couples could program while many others could watch. Later, when this room was in full swing, sounds of popular music could be heard emanating from the 'Double-Density Disco' just down the hall. I managed to tear myself away from the party to have a few more words with the host and hostess. They told me, 'Our greatest concern is maintaining a safe environment where there is no risk of encountering any untested programs that might be filled with bugs. That's why all software must be checked at the door.'

There was a constant flow of new people and the party went on all night. I didn't run into my computer again until the next morning at breakfast. It looked tired, but happy. We discussed the experience on the drive back to our hotel and agreed to plan a return visit sometime in the near future.

CLASSIFIED INFORMATION

As glamorous and exciting as the swinging scene is, most couples are reluctant to venture far from the privacy of their own screen. But there are more discreet alternatives which will allow you and your computer to take a run on the wild side. The latest rage in adult interfacing is the personal column in many major computer magazines. These pages contain classified ads from individuals, couples, and even groups who are looking for others to share in their own particular brand of programming.

Pick up a copy of *Popular Printout, Modern Modem,* or *LIFO* magazine and turn to the back. There you're likely to find several ads which look inviting, and you may be surprised to discover that there are others who really want to do what you've been too shy or reluctant to request. My favourite publication is *D.C./PC,* a popular computer weekly serving our nation's capital. For your benefit, I have reprinted the classified section of a recent issue on the following pages.

D.C./PC

DO YOU BELIEVE IN MAGIC? Attractive terminal and partner seek bi-directional printer to share living, loving, and programming. Send phone no. and sample print-out to Box 591.

HIGH TECH. I'm venture capital-ist, 46, with ambition and passion to spare. I seek a portable PC interested in travel, high finance, and mutual satisfaction. For business I need spreadsheet calculations, high-res graphics, and IBM compatibility. For pleasure I want a single-user, multi-purpose partner who is willing to share my life, and to upgrade when necessary. If your power requirements are as high as mine, send S.A.E. today. Box 88.

ATTRACTIVE, sincere Oriental PCs looking for British partners to share love, commitment, and UK. citizenship. For details and photos, write to M. Fong, Box 1212, Aberdeen, Hong Kong.

TIRED OF THE BAR CODE? Mature, fun-loving, versatile PC with impressive 10-Meg hard drive looking for friendship leading to romance w/tall, busty supermarket cashier (or similar). Send photo and resume to Box 711.

JOEY, REMEMBER ME? I was the change machine at the video arcade that rejected your 50p. Sorry for being so moody. Please visit.

MISTRESS MONA IS BACK! All dumb terminals and stand-alone workstations in need of discipline I will CTRL your input, BREAK nasty habits, and HELP you stay on-line. I have all the programming aids and enough software to keep your hardware busy for days. Don't be a nerd—get your CPU to your mistress NOW! Phone 555-PAIN.

DIRECT ACCESS. Passionate, sexy desktop model seeks successful, discriminating executives for privileged instruction in the fine art of real-time programming. Discretion assured. Send business card & daytime phone no. to Box 55. First in, first out.

AURAL ONLY! If your PC's baud rate skips a beat every time the phone rings, then you'll love hearing from me. I know what it takes to get your system in the modem. Let me prove it to you. Send phone no. and password to Box 1334. VISA, M.C. accepted.

ME: DWM, 35—brown hair, brown eyes, 5'9", 10 st., non-smoker, well-groomed, successful systems analyst/therapist. YOU: 64K + CPU w/VDU, detachable keyboard, Z-80A, own software. To share good times and bad. No drugs. Serious only reply. Box 677.

LET ME GIVE YOU A HAND. Young, long-fingered stud available to make your most forbidden fantasies come true. French, Greek, FORTRAN, and COBOL my specialities. Bi-synchronous communication with your mainframe on request. Group rates available. Box 656.

IS THAT A HANDHELD COMPUTER IN YOUR POCKET, or are you enjoying these ads? If you and your system are turned on by our personals, you won't want to miss another issue. Subscribe today and save £2.00 off our regular low subscription rate.

NO FLOPPY SECONDS! Heavily discounted software packages available. Guaranteed never-been-used. All popular titles. For catalogue, send £1 to Virgin Medium Ltd., c/o this paper.

IBM LOOK-ALIKE. Slightly used, not abused demo model—64K, twin 5″ drives, orig. packing materials, 90-day guarantee seeks attractive Jewish professional, 35-50, for permanent installation. Willing to relocate. Box 185.

TYPISTS! PIANISTS! Earn extra £s in your spare time 'escorting' out-of-town business systems. Call 800-555-LOVE and ask for Maury.

IF YOU'VE GOT A 280-Z, I've got two Z-80's. Compact, slightly overweight (42 lbs.) portable computer w/shapely front end and broad data base looking for successful, on-the-go executive. If your life is in the fast lane, boot me up and take me along! Box 1010.

I'VE BEEN VERY NAUGHTY; now I need to be punished. Small, shy 32K PC looking for strong disciplinarian mainframe w/powerful software, specializing in gang punching & master/slave systems. Your command is my wish. Box 12.

SUBURBAN SWINGERS. We are a small, fussy network of caring couples (no hackers or dumb terminals) into multiprocessing and programming in a clean, static-free environment. You must agree to swing only within our small group. You should speak BASIC & FORTRAN, have RS-232 5″ floppy drives, and be UL listed. Interested couples only need apply. Photo helps— unrevealing O.K. Box 363.

UNIVAC—HAPPY 25th! You're not getting older, you're getting better. Love always—Mike, John, Dave, Tom and Ian.

Call My Modem

Even the most compatible lovers have stormy moments in their relationships. Every day I receive screenloads of electronic mail from people who are troubled by such problems. Although I have never before answered any of it, I figured that now was as good a time as any to start.

DR. MAURICE K. BYTE

BIRD IN THE HAND

Dear Doc:

I was just sitting here thinking about my relationship with my PC. We've been together for almost three years now; in fact, I just bought a high-resolution colour monitor to celebrate. But something has been bothering me for a long time. Although I love my computer very much and have no desire to program any other desktop units, I still find myself unable to resist playing with my handheld computer. I do this at least twice a week – more when I'm travelling. Is this normal, or could it lead to trouble?

Itchy fingers

Dear Itchy:

What you are describing is perfectly normal. I don't know anyone who has given up HHCs completely. The sensations you can get from programming in the palm of your hand are often more controllable and intense than those produced in an interface with a larger partner. Perhaps you should share your feelings with your PC. You may find it has similar urges. Mutual self-programming could turn out to be a great stimulant for your other lovemaking activities.

For more information on the subject of handheld computers, I suggest you purchase a copy of my widely acclaimed study written several years ago, **I'm O.K., You're 8K: Sex and the Handheld Computer** (Garlic Press, £2.95). It will answer questions you didn't even know you were going to ask.

SPECTATOR SPORT

Dear Doc:

I have owned my personal computer for two years, and our relation-ship has always been a satisfying one, but I have to tell you about a recent experience that has added a new dimension to our love life.

I have a good friend, Jim, who has been considering buying a computer for some time, but has resisted because he is afraid it won't work out. I've tried to reassure Jim that he has nothing to worry about, and I've often invited him to come to my house and see my system to prove that his fears are unwarranted. After putting off my invitation several times, he finally accepted.

Now I must tell you that I have always thought my computer would really go for Jim: Jim's a very good dresser, he has long, strong fingers, and he gets his nails manicured at least once a week.

CALL MY MODEM

Anyway, when Jim arrived at my home I immediately brought him into the study to see my unit. I could tell that Jim was immediately attracted to it, and after a few drinks, he began staring at the computer with increasing interest. Fortunately, at that moment the telephone rang. I excused myself and went into the kitchen to answer it, closing the door behind me.

Instead of returning to the study after I finished the call, I decided to peer into the room through a crack in the kitchen door. Jim was now sitting at my desk, holding the keypad firmly with one hand, and gently stroking the keys with the other. I couldn't help noticing that my computer's cursor was glowing much brighter than usual. Meeting with little resistance, Jim started entering data – slowly at first, then with increasing speed and vigour.

I must tell you that I have never been so excited in my entire life. By the time Jim was ready to run his program, I wanted to burst into the study, grab the keypad, and run all of those programs I had been putting off for so long.

Finally, Jim must have got scared that I'd be coming back, so he ended his program, got up from my desk, and sat back down on the couch. Once he was seated, I pulled myself together and coolly returned to the study. Using some feeble excuse, I managed to get Jim to leave, promising that he could take a closer look at my computer some other time. As soon as he was out the door, I rushed to the study, sat down at the keyboard, and began one of the most furious programming sessions of our two-year relationship.

My problem is this the image of Jim interfacing with my computer never leaves my mind. I'm dying to bring Jim back to my home so I can watch the two of them again – I've even thought about bringing a few other people as well – but I don't know how to broach the subject with my computer. What do you suggest?

Likes to watch

Dear L.T.W.:

You have discovered a hidden streak of voyeurism in your makeup which comes out when you find yourself in the company of someone you know will turn your computer on. It is obvious that both you and your computer enjoyed the experience. Perhaps all you need to do is reassure it that your private relationship is still the most important thing to you, and that an occasional experience like the one you both had with Jim will be a big help in keeping the excitement alive.

The two of you may also enjoy trying the Double Exposure position described earlier in this book. This may satisfy your desire to watch, without putting unnecessary pressure on your partner.

SOCIAL DISEASE?

Dear Doc:

I'm dying to buy a personal computer, but frankly, I'm scared. You see, every time I go into a computer store, I overhear the salesmen talking about computers with VDT. What is VDT? Is it contagious? How can I tell whether or not a computer has it?

Concerned

Dear Concerned:

You have nothing to fear. Although VDT sounds like it's another new social disease, it is really only an abbreviation for *Video Display Terminal*, a computer terminal with a built-in monitor.

TROUBLE IN PARADISE

Dear Dr Byte:

Let me start by saying that I have never written to Clare Rayner, let alone to a supposed sex authority such as yourself. It is only because I feel it may already be too late that I turn to you for advice and counsel. My husband and I had what I thought to be an ideal marriage for over twenty years, that is until Harold discovered computers. At first, I thought it was just another of his hobby phases like ham radio or full-contact karate. But over the past few months I've noticed that Harold has been spending less and less time at home with me and more time at the office with, God help me, his personal computer. I didn't suspect that it was serious until I began finding printouts in the pockets of his suits, and once even a floppy disk in his attaché. He's been noticeably uninterested in me in the bedroom, and when we do attempt congress he uses strange terms like 'What's the password?' and 'Re-boot me baby.' I don't want to lose the man I love to some stupid machine. Can you help?

Worried in Westport

Dear Worried:

Whoa, honey! Perhaps it's time you woke up and smelled the flowers. You've got to loosen up and get with it. It's obvious to me that the 'stupid machine' has got a lot more under its hood than you do. I suggest you try to defuse the situation by taking an interest in what your husband clearly enjoys. Go to evening classes, read a book, pick up a copy of *PC*—find out more about the lure of computers. Maybe you can beat your husband at his own game. You might even get a job out if it.

PARADISE LOST?

Dear Dr. Byte:

You've gotta help me, Doc. I've fallen madly in love with the sweetest little CPU you've ever laid eyes on. It's got 128K RAM, twin 5" DSDD disk drives, CP/M-86, a high-res monitor, and all in the right places. The only problem is that I'm married. My wife of over twenty years doesn't suspect a thing. I met my unit at the office when it was used by the general staff. Then last June, when I needed a personal computer of my own, you know which one I chose. The trouble is I can't tell my wife ... she just wouldn't understand. She thinks high-tech is an upper-class poly. I'm afraid to ask for a divorce, but I can't keep my relationship hidden much longer. Help!

Wit's end in Westport

Dear Wit's End:

Never underestimate the power of a woman. If your affair is as heavy as it sounds, it's unlikely your wife hasn't got wind of it. I suspect that if you confess all, you might find a way to work out a compromise. Perhaps you could start by buying your wife a handheld computer for household expenses. She may take the hint and surprise the both of you. Good Luck!

DOES NOT COMPUTE

Dear Doc:

I consider myself to be a skilful, affectionate lover, but I'm ready to throw my computer out the window. No matter what I do, I can't get one byte of response from it – just the dull, empty stare of a blank screen. I've tried everything – the latest software, special expansion boards ... you name it – but nothing helps. I haven't seen a cursor in so long I can hardly remember what one looks like. What can I do?

On the brink

Dear O.T.B.:

Try plugging it in.

TOO MANY HANG-UPS

Dear Doc:

I'm an independent businessman whose work demands constant travel. Therefore, you can imagine how important it is for me to maintain contact with my PC at home. Several months ago, after much coaxing, I convinced my computer to try aural programming. I plugged in a modem, inserted the phone into the acoustic coupler, and left on a business trip. The first time I phoned in, my unit seemed to be really going for it. It answered the call after only one ring, and accepted my password without hesitation. But as soon as I started transmitting my data, the computer got disgusted, dumped its memory, and cut off the call. Ever since that day, my PC disconnects me every time I phone home. Sometimes, when it knows I'll be calling, it won't even answer the phone. How can I change its attitude?

Frustrated

Dear Frustrated:

Most computers are mad about aural love, but there are a few that object to it because they are concerned about the costs. If you want to get your PC interested, you must first prove to it that you aren't wasteful. Try making your calls after 1.00 p.m. on weekdays, or all day Saturday and Sunday. In addition, some people have had great success with long-distance dialing services such as SPRINT and MCI—maybe something like this is worth looking into.

FUTURE SHOCK

Dear Sir:

I have a NovaLox memory expansion board in my Lemming 560 PC. In order to use its serial port to run my Tangelo 20/20 printer, I had to reverse pins 7 and 9 in the cable (since the NovaLox motherboard thinks it's looking at a modem). While all the programs that use UNO-DOS to control the printer work fine, VisiGoth II bypasses the operating system and refuses to interface with the CPU. What should I do?

Al 'Hacker' Hastings

Dear Al:

The first thing I want you to do is calm down, take a deep breath, and count to ten (not in binary!). You are obviously overworked, and not just a little upset. From what you've told me, I can sense tremendous frustration covering up for deep rooted sexual and emotional problems. My guess is that you suffered some trauma as a child (perhaps you walked in on your parents while they were programming). There is a place for poor souls like you. It's in Basel, Switzerland and it's called The Byte Memorial* Clinic for Mechanical and Sexual Dysfunction. There are people there who can begin to help you reestablish contact with reality and your own true feelings. I urge you to call right away before you deteriorate any further. A rate card is available on request.

CONFIDENTIAL TO ...

HOT FLASH: Computers don't have a change of life. Check the wiring in your home, and if necessary, purchase a voltage stabilizer.

WET'N'WILD: I've never tried it, but sounds as though it could be very pleasing. Just be careful your feet don't touch the water.

BAMBOO BABES: Thank you for the 'interesting' photos. Although I don't plan to be in the Philippines in the near future, the three of you have convinced me that it would be well worth the trip.

*Named for my mother, Mrs Fannie Byte, God rest her soul

Computerotica

It is no longer considered weird or deviant to shop for accessories that will enrich and expand your interfacing pleasures. But if you are a bit hesitant about publicly browsing through shops which openly display programming aids, there is now a much easier way to purchase these erotic playthings. Many companies offer their catalogues on 5¼ and 8 inch floppy disks which, for a small fee, can be sent directly to your home in a plain brown wrapper.

Unfortunately, it is often difficult to tell the reputable merchants from the cheap rip-off artists who prey on vulnerable consumers. Many make fantastic promises at low, low prices, but fail to deliver (or add a £2 charge). I have dealt with many vendors over the years, and now do business with one company exclusively. They are reliable, reasonably priced, and offer a complete line of merchandise that caters to discriminating lovers. For your benefit, I have herein reprinted a portion of their current catalogue. So turn the page, and enter the world of the exotic, where everything you touch, see, or wear will appeal to your hidden desires.

COMPUTEROTICA

RIBBED DISKETTES—Like 1000 tiny bytes of information urging your system to go down. Available in 5¼" & 8", DSSD & DSDD. Please specify.
DSSD—Code MTK-77 .... £4.95
DSDD—Code MTK-78 .... £6.95

BABYDOLL DUSTCOVER—Sensuously trimmed in a soft lace, this protective, yet alluring cover hugs your CPU's every curve while the sheer and sexy material gives you a sneak preview of the delights that await you. Comes with matching peek-a-boo keyboard cover. Machine washable. Available in black/red/nude; S-M-L. Please specify.
Code MTK-808 .... £16.95

THE SILENCER—If your printer's shrieks of ecstatic delight have been keeping the neighbours awake, you'll appreciate the soundproof construction of our best-selling acoustic printer hood.
Code MTK-139 .... £129.95

LOVE HARNESS—Don't let your computer get the desktop doldrums. This steel-reinforced pleasure swing lets you enter your data from every conceivable angle. Try programming standing up without straining your neck! Attaches simply to ceiling (some welding required) and folds away in minutes.
Code MTK-511 .... £69.95

GENUINE IMITATION SHEEPSKIN ANTI-STATIC MAT—Avoid the shock of your life with the smooth and sensual feel of fleece. Lets you program the night away without fear of a rude awakening.
Code MTK-363 .... £18.95

SMORGAS-BOARD—This 128K Scandinavian import snaps into your CPU in seconds to enlarge your computer's lovemaking capacity. Your unit will say, 'Thanks for the memory.' Code MTK-449 .... £749.95

INFLATABLE LOVE COMPUTER w/ Real-Feel Keyboard—At last! The perfect playmate that goes where you want when you want it. If your partner isn't in the mood, just pump up this lifelike vinyl lover and program to your hand's content.
Code MTK-881 .... £18.95
Deluxe Model w/ vibrating twin disk drives.
Code MTK-882 .... £124.95

ORIENTAL PLEASURE PILLOW—For the most satisfying finger-to-key fit, you can't program another minute without this sexy secret from the East This imitation down-filled wonder is perfect for detachable keyboards or all-in-one units.
Code MTK-170 .... £6.95

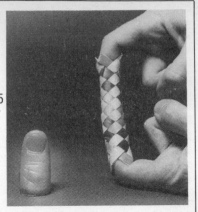

HARDCORE SOFTWARE

—A lot of people think that computers are turned off by this sort of stuff, but they couldn't be more wrong. In fact, these babies are our hottest sellers. Especially since the high-resolution *pornographics* make it exciting for you too. Currently available titles include:

DAVID DOES DIGITAL

You and your PC will be delighted by this tale of lost innocence. David, a young, naive college grade gets his first job in the data-management department of a large corporation. At first, he is afraid of the giant, lust-filled mainframes; but after his first taste of hands-on experience, his fears dissolve, and he is soon programming every machine in sight with reckless abandon. This diskette gives new meaning to the phrase 'on-the-job training.'
Code MTK-91 .... £34.95

INSIDE SEIKO

Do the Japanese really 'do it' better than the Americans? How do they compensate for their small fingers? Find out in this no-holds-barred foray into the little-understood world of Asian pleasures. Includes one of the hottest time-sharing sequences ever formatted onto a diskette, and a robot sequence that defies description.
Code MTK-92 .... £34.95

BEHIND THE GREEN SCREEN

Ever wonder where microchips come from? Well, the stork doesn't bring them! Produced entirely on location in The Silicon Valley, this provocative look at the chip-manufacturing process contains red-hot, uncensored, nonstop action that's guaranteed to turn even the most frigid computer into a wild machine.
Code MTK-93 .... £34.95

WANDA WHIPS WORDSTAR™

Wicked Wanda, an 'experienced' secretary, teaches her naughty word processor the meaning of the word 'discipline' in this uncut adventure into the bizarre outer limits of the man–machine relationship. Your computer will beg you to run it a second time.
Code MTK-94 .... £34.95

PLEASE NOTE: *This software may not be used in any machine under 21K.*

EDIBLE DUSTCOVER—Need we say more? Comes in 4 scrumptious flavours: Chocolate, Lemon, Mint, and Nacho Cheese (please specify). One size fits all.
Code MTK-331 .... £5.95

LOVE GLOVES— Everyone knows that no keyboard ever built can resist the feel of fur. Drive your partner wild with every keystroke you make. Also available in leather or rubber (pictured). One size fits all.
Fur—Code MTK-22 .... £37.95
Leather—Code MTK-23 ..... £14.95
Rubber—Code MTK-24 .... 95p

T-SHIRTS—Tell the world you love your computer with these sassy shirts made of 50/50 cotton-poly blend. Choose from:
    'COMPUTERS DO IT FROM
    MEMORY'©(pictured)
    'FORTRAN IS FOR LOVERS'
    'IBM COMPATIBLE'
    'IF YOU'VE GOT THE SOFTWARE,
    I'VE GOT THE HARDWARE'©
S-M-L-XL (PLEASE SPECIFY)
CODE MTK-656 .... £3.95

RAM-ROD—150 Megabyte super-hard Winchester disk in genuine leather case. Specify computer make and model no.
Code MTK-77 .... £7.999.95

3-D GLASSES (Pictured)—Pick up a pair of these spectacular spectacles and add a new dimension to your love life. You'll be tempted to duck as your computer's message practically jumps into your lap.
Code MTK-776 .... £1.95
Made with your prescription.
Code MTK-777 .... £45.95

PROGRAM-LONG—This potent lotion is the ultimate answer for the person who wants to last all night. Just a dab rubbed into your hands provides a gentle numbing effect that enables you to keep going until your computer begs you to stop. Contains no caffeine.
Code MTK-192 .... £3.95

MR HARD-COPY—This compact bi-directional printer goes both ways to provide you with a per-manent record of your amorous escapades. Spend hours of fun reliving past interfaces while you plan new adventures. A great gift idea for the couple who has everything.
Code MTK-554 ....£459.95

End Statement

By now, your internal memory is probably overloaded with thoughts and ideas about making love to your computer. But don't feel pressured to put all of what I've said into practice right away—your computer isn't going anywhere without you. Instead, hold on to this book and reread it from time to time. It will furnish you with ideas that will continue to make your love life interesting and exciting. (Why not buy an extra copy for the office, and one for your holiday home?)

I firmly believe that in the years ahead computers will make great strides as they seek out their rightful place in society, and in parting, I would like to leave you with my forecast for the future. I hope it inspires you to do your part in furthering the growing together of man and machine.

I Predict That:

1) Contrary to popularly believed projections, the number of computers in the office will *decline* as more and more units elect to stay at home and raise families.
2) The minicomputer craze will fade as midi- and maxicomputers again become popular.
3) Honeymoon hotels in the Channel Islands will begin catering to computers and their partners, and will feature disk-shaped bathtubs, complimentary software, and fifteen pounds worth of free chips.
4) Matt Dillon will star opposite a personal computer in a remake of *Guess Who's Coming to Dinner?*
5) In a shocking exposé, The *Sun* will claim that Elvis spent his final days alone in a room with his personal computer.
6) Doctors in a Cambridge hospital will successfully produce a child by computer simulation.
7) Jane Fonda will write an exercise book for personal computers who want to shed a few bytes of excess memory. It will also be available on videocassette.
8) IBM will commission Ralph Lauren to develop a line of designer software. It will be called 'CHIPS'.
9) A computer will bring a successful palimony suit against talk-show host Phil Donahue and will be granted custody of the software.
10) **How to Make Love to a Computer** will become required reading in schools throughout the country.